Copyright © 2007 by Cassandra L. Thomas

Printed and bound in the United States of America. Published by Butterfly Publications. All rights reserved. No part of this publication may be reproduced or transmitted in any form or by any means, electronic or mechanical, including but not limited to photocopying, recording, or by any information storage and retrieval system, without the written permission from the publisher.

Requests for permission to make copies of any part of this work should be emailed to:

Cassandra L. Thomas
Permission Requests
booksavenuemagazine@yahoo.com

This book is a work of fiction. Names, characters, businesses, organizations, places, events, and incidents either are the product of the author's imagination or are used fictitiously. Any resemblance to actual persons, living or dead, events, or locales is entirely coincidental.

A beautiful adult love story written in a down home storytelling dialect about a young girl (SNOOKIE) who falls head over hills for a guitar player at a local juke joint. But hold on to your seat as (TILLIE) sturs up a world of trouble that eventually back fire. Filled with juke joint laughter, heart wrenching moments, challenges, praises, forgiveness, love and healing. If you enjoy reading books by Zora Neal Hurston, Toni Morrison, Alice Walker, Maya Angelou & J. California Cooper to name a few, then you will surely enjoy A Wonderful Place. Sit back and curl up near your fireplace, on your screened-in porch or in your favorite chair, and allow this story to take you to that special place.

Aknowledgements

All praise and honor to God for blessing me with an imagination since my early years. I thank the beautiful small town of Culloden, Georgia where my roots began for inspiring my imagination. My late Grandmother, Annie Maude Smith-Thomas for her love, spirit, wisdom and many, many remedies. My one hundred and one year old grandfather, The late Reverend Ben Ramey for your teachings, wisdom, protection & unconditional love. My paternal Grandmother, Vannie P. Smith for your disciplinary, love, spirit, wisdom and many, many remedies. My late Grandfather, Sam Denson, Sr. for your kind & gentle spirit. My great Aunties and Uncles (Annie Clyde, Annie Bell, Sanders, Aunt Louise, Uncle Benny, Aunt Domp, Aunt Lilah Mae, Uncle T, Uncle Rich, Uncle Alford, Uncle BH, Uncle David "Jr." Pennamon). The entire Smith, Barnes, Thomas & Pennamon family whom I am happy to honor in this book, my beautiful late mother, Johnnie Mae Thomas-Plummer for loving me in a special way & teaching me to embrace my roots. My Great-Grandmother, the late Mollie Smith and my Great, Great-Grandmother, the late Francis Barnes whom we all are descendants of. My son, Dexter R. Thomas for your love and support, My siblings, Temetress Martin, Candace Morton, Donna, Jan, Diane, Paul, Ronnie, Samuel & Julian. Mrs. Robbie Bronner for your down home spirit. Sol Factor Band, (Phil, Ryan, Dave, Raheem, Mike & Tahnee) I dedicate this book to all of you for always taking my heart to...a wonderful place.

*To Michael,
May the hammer of success knock the hell out of you! I'm proud of you. Stay focus. Much love & Blessings
Cassandra L. Thomas*

A Wonderful Place

Chapter 1

"Come on hea Snookie, we gon miss de band!" **She hollered**. *"Don't be rushin me Essie, I don't know why I let you talk me into comin to dis place anyhow. I should be at home git'n ready to cook biscuits fa my brothas and sistahs in de moning. I hope my mama is busy doin sump'n fa de Lawd up in heaven tonite, so she caint see me up in a Juke Joint"*. **I complained** *"Chile please, let de dead bury de dead, now come on hea."* **Us paid fifty-cents to git in, then she grabbed my hand and pulled me through de doorway. Eb'body in town must hav been there.**

De smell of fried fish, fried red links, fried chicken and hot dogs wuz in de air, peeple wuz dancin, laughin, kissin and everthang. She did all dat fussin jes to see foe men sit'n on a stage, dat sat

low in de corner of a room playin off tune, I's thankin to myself. Dey had a drumma, slim yella man dat woe a big hat where you couldn't see his eyes, a big brown skinned piano playa dat couldn't stay in his seat on de count of him git'n up every now and then, dancin wit his shoes off while he played dat piano. I can tell de women jes loved him, cause he a good lookin man. One of'em even had a washboard dat he wuz scratchin wit sum kinda object, but there wuz only one dat stood out in de soul of my eyes. He wuz playin de guitar, and he made his fangers do tricks wit those strangs too. He wuz showin out, you hea me? I's thankin every thang bout dis band wuz terrible till my eyes met his. Big ole man witta bald head and smooth caramel color to him. He had brown eyes dat looked like a pretty shiny button, and a smile dat could wake de

sun up. *"Essie, who dat?"* **I pointed at him.** *"Oh dat's Big Ben, he de only one dat ain't went out wit anybody hea, sum say he too uppity fa his-self. And sides, he younger than you,"* **I's leaning back in my chair wit my arms folded. Dat ain't whut I's feelin from Big Ben, he seemed mo like a gentle man to me; shy and different from de others. I's member when Essie wuz goin witta younger man long foe she met Tim. Head strong fa him too, made me never wanna hav a younga man fa myself. But I's like dis fella, and I wunda if he even know whut to do witta woman like me...a virgin. Maybe it wuz meant fa me to be hea tonite since I don't never go nowhere. Been taking care of my siblings since mama and daddy died. Never stopped to thank once dat I wuz missin sumpn in my life, and dat sumpn wuz a big strong man. And now dat de subject don come up, I's reckon**

I's gon wait and see whut de end gon be.

Big Ben walked ova to our table while dey wuz taking a break. *"Hey Miss Essie, how you be tonite?"* **He asked.** *I's be jes fine Big Ben, how you be?"* **She asked him back.** *"Jes fine, jes fine."* **There he go wakin up de sun wit dat pretty smile, I's thankin to myself.** *"Big Ben, dis hea is my best friend Snookie, she don't git out much so I's cided dat I's gon treat'er out tonite,"* **Essie tole him.** *"How you doin Miss Snookie?"* **He greeted me.** *"Hay, how you doin?"* **I said witta smile. Our eyes locked fa a moment and fire rushed through my heart as his eyes glazed at mine. Sump'n bout de feelin I's git'n from him made me wunda if he de one, caint explain de feelin I's jes got but I's knowed dat sump'n there.**

I laid still in de darkness of my room and thought about how us had a good time at de juke joint. And then my thoughts slipped ret on to Big Ben befoe I's fell off to sleep.

"Dear God, somehow I feel dat you sent me to dat place tonite fa a reason. Could it be Lawd dat you want me to be wit a musician even though daddy always said dat life witta musician won't work? Sho me Lawd whut yo will is in dis cause I don't wanna do nuthin gainst yo will. Feelins sturd up in me like never befoe bout dis man. Forgiv me if I's wrong bout all of dis, Amen."

Big Ben wuz on my mind ever second of de day. I woke up thankin bout'em, I thought about'em while I's cooking breakfast, lunch, and suppa. I could hardly eat fa thankin bout'em, I went to bed thankin bout'em. I's thankin how us sho can use a big strong man like him round dis hea house, but most of all; I's sho need fa sumbody other than my folks to love me and I's lov'em ret back.

Wunda whut it feels like to hav sumbody love ya? Reckon I's know one day. I tell ya one thang, I's never missed goin to dat Juke Joint since dat furst nite. Even though I wuz git'n tied of goin, I wanted Big Ben to see me ova all de other women and I wanted him to come calling on me. I wanted to cook fa him but I didn't know how to invite him ova fa suppa cause I really

ain't never knowed a man I wanted to cook fa, seemed like he didn't notice me anyhow.

Chapter 2

Ever nite afta we fed de chullins, baze dem and put'em to bed, Auntee Johnnie Mae and me sat on de screened-in poach burnin ole rags to keep de mosquitos away, lookin up at de stars and talkin. She tole me stories bout my mama and her when they wuz yungons. Older folks always talked bout how many miles they had to walk to school back then. I's thankin bout tellin her bout my visits to de juke joint cause far as I's know, didn't nobody know bout me goin.

"Snookie, when is you gon git yoself another sofa chair?" **Auntee Johnnie Mae asked me in her deep southern high pitched voice as she opened de screened door steppin onto de poach holdin a pitcha of cold lemonade wit ice and sliced lemons in it.** *"I ain't thought about it much Auntee, dat*

one feels so good to sleep on". **I said to her witta smile.** *"Well I'll ask Miss Edgewood if she know of anybody who's lookin to throw their's out anytime soon cause dat jes don't make no sense atall!"* **Auntee Johnnie Mae is a fancy lady, fancy than most others in town. Her house look jes like de houses dat she clean sumtimes cause de white folks don giv'er whut dey don't want no mo. She don't really hav to work cause she got money dat grandmamma and my folks left her. She hea wit me mo than she at her own house cause I'm her sistah's chile and she knowed I wuz gon need sumbody to holp me wit my two sistahs and my two brothas. I jes ack like I didn't even hea her blabbin at de mouth while I's cut'n me a slice of de lemon pound cake dat wuz already sittin on de round wood table next to my chair.** *"Auntee Johnnie Mae, hav you ever had a*

man dat played in a band?" **I asked.**
"Naw chile, you don't want no man dat play in a band cause dey hav too many women at'em. Sum of these men hav sum weak souls, dey means well but dey always seems to let de other head do all de talkin if you know whut I mean." **She said.**
"Well, Essie took me to de Juke Joint wit her two Fridays ago and I's been goin back ever since, **I said to her.**
"Whaaaaat, Lawd'a mussy. I know yo mama and daddy is jes rollin ova in dey graves to hea you say dat!" **She screamed.** "Oh Auntee it won't bad as I thought it wuz gon be, jes calm yo self down foe you giv yo self a heart attack!" **I screamed back.**
"Well I suppose you rite," **she said in a mo calmer tone as she cut herself a slice of cake.** To tell de truth, yo mama and me use to hit dem juke joints ever weekend back in our day, and as quiet as it's kept. Dats where she met yo daddy." **My eyes widened as she looked at me wit dat ole slick smile of**

hers. *"I met a man dat plays de guitar there by de name of Big Ben. I know dat I only seent him a few times but I's got dis feelin in my soul bout'em,"* **I tole *her*. She looked at me wit care in her eyes like mama use to do when she wuz worried bout me.** *"Snookie, chile de man dat God wants you to be wit is gon find you, don't you go out there lookin fa no man cause if ya do, you'll jes git yo self hurt. Now take it from a woman wit experience. You's still young chile and you hav plenty of time fa love."* **She said wit her wisdom.** *"I ain't forgot whut you, mama and grandmamma taught me. I ain't gon go afta him, but I sho want'em to notice me and to come afta me. How can I git'em to see me Auntee ova all dem other women?"* **I pleaded to her.** *"De only reason why I's been goin back ever week is cause I want him to say sump'n to me furst. I know dat all dis goin out is gon wear off soon. I wanna talk to him away from dat place in private* *so I can git to know de person who he really is."* **She jes looked at me and said,** *"Furst of all gal, if you hav to make him notice you, then he probably ain't de one fa ya. If God meant fa you to be wit dis Big Ben, it'll happen, you jes wait."* **I sat there quiet, listenin to my Auntee. I wish Big Ben knowed how my heart ached fa him. One time he kissed me on de cheek as he walked round de room and said sump'n sweet to me all at de same time. Chile I couldn't eat fa days cause I's all de time thankin bout whut he did and said. And jes thank, I made such a big fuss to Essie bout draggin me to dat place and now I caint stop goin on de count of me bein sweet on him. She sho wuz rite bout one thang, I's never saw Big Ben leave dat juke joint witta woman. I hea talk dat he works in ole man Kirkwood's field everday pickin potatoes and sumtimes building shelves fa his pantry.**

Dey say a man sumtime brang worry, dats jes how I's feelin rite about now. Auntee Johnnie Mae jes looked at me and said in her sweet voice. *"Like I said, if God tends fa you to be wit dis Big Ben, nuthin in dis whole world can stop it. You jes keep prayin and askin him to lead you in de rite direction."* **And then she opened up her big brown arms fa me to come to her and she gav me de hardest hug.**

Chapter 3

I thought about my Auntee as I's walkin down Smith and Barnes ole rocky road, it wuz a clear pretty Friday. She went to de doctor dis moning so I took her place at work. I don't thank Miss Edgewood is gon let me come back to cook and clean fa her again when Auntee Johnnie Mae caint make it cause I burnt one of her brothas white shirts. She had dat good music goin and I couldn't help but t git lost in it, and then Big Ben came to my mind and honeychile I jes forgot all about whut I's doin. It's been five months now since I's been goin.

Essie wuz sittin on de poach when I got to de house. *"Hay girl,"* She said as I took a seat next to her. *"Hay girl, I's tied and I don't thank I's goin back to dat place cause I burnt one of Miss Edgewood brotha's shirt."* **I tried to sound concern bout it but I couldn't cause Essie knows me betta than anybody.** *"Po Miss Ole Edgewood brotha's shirt,"* **she said witta sad face dat tole me dat she didn't bit mo care bout no shirt than I did, and then us jes looked at one nother and bust out in laughter.** *"Did my Auntee git back from de doctor yet?"* **I asked her** *"Naw not yet,"* **she answered. De kids came runnin from behind de house, Lil Billy's pants wuz wet.** *"Come hea lil Billy,"* **I said calmly. He had a silly sad look on his face cause he knowed he wuz gon git it. He wuz eight years old now and he knew betta to be pissin in his clothes.** *"How come you didn't go to dat bathroom?"* **I asked him.** *"I couldn't hole it."* **He whined.** *"Stop dat whinning boy and go git me a switch."* **He went to de side of de house and came back wit a teeny weeny skinny switch, and dat made me even madder.** *"Flo, go* *git me a switch and let it be a good one to. He know betta to be brangin me dis ole lil biddy switch,"* **I said to my sistah who's almost twelve years in age now.** *"Kay!"* **She hollered back, I can tell she wuz glad to go fetch me dat switch, but if it wuz her gittin de whuppin she'd be hiding sumwhere. I whupped him real good and sent him in de house fa de rest of de day, ole piss cat.** *"Yonda come yo Auntee,"* **Essie pointed toward de direction where Auntee Johnnie Mae wuz walkin down de dirt road carryin a bag. We stood up and headed in her direction.** *"You goin to de juke joint tonite?"* **She asked me.** *"Chile you know I's gotta see Big Ben tonite, seems like Fridays caint git hea fast enough,"* **I said.** *"Hav he asked you out yet?"* **She asked as she bucked dem big cat eyes of hers.** *"No chile, he don't even notice I'm there. Sides, he may not even like my kind anyhow,"* **I said.** *"And* whut kind is you Snookie?" **She asked.** "I'm dark skinned my hips and stomach too big, and he even might like dem ole high yella gals like you anyhow." **She stopped walkin and grabbed me by de shoulders and turned me in her direction and scawled me good.** "Now you listen hea Snookie Brown, you's a pretty gurl and everbody likes you. Men jes ain't as fast as we are, dey likes to take dey time and make sho dey know whut dey gittin dey self into. He likes you cause I sees de way he looks at you. Don't ever let me hea you puttin yo self down like dat no mo, you hea?" **She glazed in my eyes.** "Yea I hea, I'll be ready early dis time so we can git a good seat," **I smiled.** "Dat's my gurl," **she said witta smile and walked away.** "Hay Miss Johnnie Mae, how you today?" **Essie greeted her.** "Jes fine Essie how you?" **Auntee Johnnie Mae returned de greeting.** "I's fine thank you, tell ya ma I say hay." **Auntee Johnnie**

Mae said to her. *"Okay I will!"* **I grabbed de bag dat she wuz carryin to lift de load off of her.** *"Hay, whut de Doctor say?"* **I asked.** *"I'm strong and healthy."* **She said witta big smile.** *"Praise de Lawd!"* **I said as I threw my free hand up in de air.** *"Praise de Lawd!"* **I don't know whut I's do wit out my Auntee, we so close and I's love her so much.**

I fixed sum Sloppy Joe sandwiches fa de chilren wit sum french fries, made sho dey got a wome bath aftawards and put'em to bed. *"Lil Billy, you betta git yo tail up and go to dat bathroom tonite cause I'ma whup you if you pee de bed, you hea me?"* **I scawled him.** *"Yes sistah,"* **he answered back.**

I wuz ready early jes like I tole Essie I wuz gon be. I wore my white dress wit de lace at de hem. Us got there jes in time to git sum good seats too. Essie invited Charlotte and Vette to come long wit us tonite, most of de time it's jes me her and ole Tillie. Tillie got all of us by eight years in age, I tole dem dey can have any man in dat band dey saw fit cept fa de guitar playa, us all laughed. I noticed a holp wanted sign sittin in de winda when us got to Mollie's tonite, dey need sumbody to clean de place up befoe dey open. I went to Mollie bout de job. She tole me dat she jes needed sumbody fa dis weekend while her other girl wuz outta town, I cepted and took de job.

We had another Friday nite of good times. And I wuz back to fill in fa Mollie's girl by six o'clock de next nite. Big Ben's band didn't play on Saturdays, he filled in fa one of de dishwashers at Mollie's de same nite I did, and I thought to myself, now ain't dat sump'n? Turns out, Big Ben and Mollie wuz kin to one nother. And befoe de nite wuz ova, I wuz holpin him wash and dry dishes. He didn't say much atall, de only time he said mo than two words wuz when we wuz setting de tables fa de breakfast crowd. He suggested dat de glasses be turned down instead of up, course I agreed wit'em; anything fa Big Ben honeychile.

Sunday nite wuz jes de same as Saturday. Mollie paid me fifty dollars fa de two days dat I worked. Big Ben wuz still quiet. I caint believe he dis quiet when he ack such a fool on stage.

I laid in de darkness of my room listenin to de sound of de house settlin and de churpin of a cricket wishin dat it would hop on sumwhere else. Won't long befoe my mind drifted to Big Ben.

"Sump'n bout him...dis man. I vowed dat I would never fool witta man in a band, but there's sump'n bout him dat makes me feel whole when us in de same room together. Sump'n bout'em dat moves me. He handsum, mature, humble, talented, smart, and sumtime silly. De sound of his voice makes my heart beat fast. I wanna know mo bout'em. Wunda if he can tell dat I's sweet on him. I's care bout'em..dis hea man, but I's Sked to git wit'em, Sked dat I mite like it. Sked dat he'll jes want my innocence, sked dat it will be good. Sked dat afta feelins and emotions git in me, he ain't gon want me no mo. Traditions says dat I caint go afta him, cause if he like me he'll come afta me.

I wanna kiss'em so bad, wit passion. How could dis be, dis love jones dat I hav fa him? I vowed dat I would never git involved witta man in a band. But there's sump'n bout big fine ass Ben." **I thought out loud as I fell off to sleep. I jumped up outta my sleep cause I's dreamin dat I's havin relations wit Big Ben. I don't even know whut it feels like to hav relations, but it sounds like sump'n good de way Essie talk about it. I's never thought about it cause I been so busy raisin these chullins. Dat dream got sump'n sturd up in me. Whew! Mussy, I might as well git on up and start on de biscuits for breakfast.**

I could hardly look Big Ben in de eyes while he played de next week. One of de waiters gav me a note dat nite, it wuz from Big Ben.

"Dear Snookee, (he spelled my name wrong) I'm not good at proachin no woman, specially one as quiet as you. I wanna talk ta ya afta de show if it's okay wit cha. If it's okay wit cha jes meet me outside."

Ben

My heart wuz beatin so fast I's thankin I's gon hav a heart attack. *"Whut de matter Snookie, you ack like you jes saw sump'n dead."* **Essie said.** *"Big Ben want me to meet'em outside afta de sho tonite."* **I smiled.** *"See there, and you wuz worrin yo pretty head fa nuthin."* **She smiled back.**

Even though one of his strangs wuz missin, Big Ben played dat guitar and dis time when he walked round de room, he came to me and stood staring at me so long; I got a lil shame faced wit eb-body lookin on and all. It made me feel like us had a connection wit one nother, but most of all it made me feel like I had a special place in his heart, and at dat moment I's thankin bout whut my daddy always said about goin out witta man in a band but I couldn't holp but to giv my heart to Big Ben cause it wuz mo than jes dat guitar dat I's love bout'em. Sump'n bout'em dat wuz speakin to me from deep down.

I's waited outside of de juke joint while Big Ben and de rest of de fellas packed up everthang. Essie dem wuz waitin in de car fa me, Roy wuz gon take us home.

Eb-body finally came out de juke joint. My body wuz shakin all ova as Big Ben walked up to me. *"Hay,"* **he said.** *"Hay,"* **I said back.** *"I jes wanted to know if you wanna go fishin wit me dis Sunday?"* **He asked me.** *"It'll hav to be afta church"* **I said.** *"I understand, can you meet me hea?"* **he asked.** *"Yeah, I be hea round two o'clock."* **I said witta smile and a sked heart all at de same time.** *"Okay, see you then."* **He tipped his hat a little while wearin dat smile I like and walked away.**

I couldn't git in de car good fa Essie dem jump'n on me wit questions. *"Whut he want witcha Snookie?"* **Essie asked.** *"He jes wanna know if I wanna go fishin wit'em Sunday afta church."* **I tole dem**. *"Whut chall gon do?"* **Tillie asked.** *"Well I's reckon us gon fish and talk Tillie, why you ask a fool question like dat fa?* **I frowned at'er.** *"Cause Miss Snookie, ever time* *a girl go down to dat pond to fish, dey ends up comin back a woman, and I hea tale dat you ain't no woman yet,"* **She said teasing me wit dat tomboy voice, Tillie's day jes ain't rite less'n she steppin on sumbody's toes, she make me siiiick!** *"Ain't yo bizness if I's a woman or not Tillie Shoemaker,"* **I snapped at'er wit my eyes wide, Essie jumped in.** *"Yall stop dat, stop it ret now, ain't no use in losin friendship ova a man!"* **Us both agreed wit Essie as de car pulled up in de yard. Auntee Johnnie Mae wuz sittin on de poach as usual.** *"Hay Miss Johnnie Mae!"* **Dey waved. Auntee Johnnie Mae threw her hands up at'em as dey drove off. I kissed her on de cheek befoe I went in de house.** *"You like goin to dat juke joint huh?"* **she asked me.** *"Jes sump'n to do on Fridays Auntee since I's never do nuthin; but don't worry, it ain't gon git de best of me,"* **I said in a sassy way wit my lips turned up.** *"Don't* *you git sassy wit me gal. I's gon sleep at my house tonite, see you in de moning."* **She lifted herself from de chair and stepped slowly down each step and wuz outta site. She jes lived next door, but de houses had a heep of space tween dem.**

I's up early de next moning wearin mama's ole yella house coat gatherin eggs from de chicken coop, dem baby chicks wuz runnin all ova de place. I cooked a big breakfast fa my siblings and sent dem outside to clean de yard while I's cleaned de house real good. I scrubbed de walls, washed windows, and I got rid of all de spider webs dat wuz clingin in ever corner of de ceilings.

It wuz a good Saturday moning, I even hung de curtains dat Auntee Johnnie Mae gav me months ago. By de end of de day us had picked a good bunch of fresh collards from de garden dat she and mama started years ago. Us make a lil money sellin sum of de vegetables, but it ain't like us need de money. My Great-Grand-daddy worked hard and saved up a heep of money befoe he died. Then my Grand-daddy and Grand-mama worked hard to add mo to it, been like dat fa years. Reason bein is so dat de next generations won't have to suffa hard as my Great-Grand-daddy did. Us jes go on makin our own money like it ain't there fa us. Auntee Johnnie Mae wuz in de kitchen preparing butta beans wit dat meat she bought from de market. It's been a family tradition to cook Sunday suppa on Saturdays. So when church is ova, all us hav to do is cook de hot wawter cone bread. Us even make de lemonade on Saturdays so dat de lemon flava can be settled in by Sunday's suppa.

I didn't pay much tention in church cause I wuz too busy writing down questions dat I wanted to ask Big Ben while us at de pond. I wuz nervous bout losin my words cause I thought dat if I lose my words, he might wannna make a woman outta me, and I's sho won't ready fa dat. As soon as service wuz ova, I rushed back to de house to eat a little and then I changed into sum ole clothes and headed fa de juke joint walkin to meet'em where us said us gon meet.

De moment I stepped past de trees, I saw him sittin on de poach of de juke joint. He wuz wearin sum ole jeans, big boots, a dark orange t-shirt and a big hat. He smiled as I proached him. *"Hay,"* I said. He tipped his hat a little. *"Hay Snookie, you all set?"* He asked me. *"Yeah"* I said. De pond wuz bout ten feet from de juke joint. He lead me to a tree near de pond dat already had fish plates wit fries sittin nice and pretty on a quilt. Confused, I asked. *"Whut's dis Big Ben?"* He smiled a little. *"De fish won't biting much, so I paid Mollie to cook us up sump'n."* De thang dat took my heart de most bout whut he did wuz dat he had fresh daisies and sunflowers sittin next to my plate. I wunda how in de world did he know I like daisies and sunflowers? *"Dis is real nice Big Ben,"* I said. *"Snookie please, don't call me Big Ben,"* Shocked, I asked. *"Well ain't dat yo name?"* He laughed. *"Dats whut de boys started callin me and then ebbody else. My real name is Benjamin Neal Phillips, but you can call me Ben."* He made me nervous starin at me de way he did. *"Okay, Ben."* I said.

Seem like us sat unda dat tree and talked fa hours git'n to know one nother. He tole me all about his life and how he watched his Grand-Daddy git a beatin from de KKK when he wuz a small boy. He have a sistah who he calls Bay-Sis. He like animals, he likes chilrens, he got a small car dat he drive when his mama wanna go shoppin in Forsyth or Atlanta, and he got two horses. He twenty-foe years old, which makes me five years older than him, and he build his own house wit his daddy on his daddy's land, he a real nice man.

De lightnin bugs wuz flyin round by de time us headed home. And by de time us got to de house, I could hea de crickets and de barks of dogs far away. He gav me a long hard hug, I tole him to be careful on his walk home. I wuz so glad Auntee Johnnie Mae had put de food up and cleaned de kitchen fa me. De Chullins musta woe her out cause she wuz sleepin soundly on de sofa chair. I took a long bath and thought about Ben de rest of de nite as usual, I could smell him on my blouse.

Chapter 4

June finally rolled around. Ben and me wuz still goin to de meetin place. Sumtimes I sat wit my back gainst de tree while he lay his head in my lap and play his guitar softly fa me. He still ain't made me a woman yet, sumtimes I wunda if he see me in dat way. I's member de furst kiss, it wuz jes a peck on de mouth. I melted rite in his arms and then I went home and cried like a baby cause it feel good when you can feel sumbody feelin you.

Essie, Tillie and me took a job pickin peaches in Roberta County on de count of it wuz git'n close to de big pot luck on de second Sunday in July. De holidays wuz comin too, and de big Second Annual Western Festival is in February. It wuz so hot out, so us had to wear gread big ole hats, long sleeve shirts and a pair of old jeans on de count of all de fur from de peaches. De peaches wuz five cents a bucket. Us needed to buy fabrics to make our costumes fa de festival, plus Mollie is havin a big party at de juke joint on Valentine nite. So dat mean I gotta make me at least three dresses. Us made a huned and fifty dollars pickin those peaches and oooo wee us scratched all de way home from dat furand when I's got there I headed straight to de tub too.

As I sat in de steamin hot wawter mixed wit sum Epson Salt. I stared out da winda into de clouds and thought about Ben and how it wuz gon be when he made me a woman.

(Four days later)

I's thankin bout how I's gon giv Ben de letter dat I wrote to him last nite as we sat unda our tree, us won't sayin much today. He jes sat there pickin at his guitar strangs while I's looking into his eyes smiling, I could tell dat sump'n wuz on his mind. I's figure its gon be now or never, so I jes pulled de letter outta my pocket and gav it to him.

"Dear Benjamin,

I believe dat de deepest connection dat two human being can hav wit one nother is de union of dey bodies. You my furst, so dis nite I's giv you all dat I's hav and all of who I is. De feelins dat I's got fa you goes beyond love, to a wonderful place. My love fa you is supreme, be gentle wit my flower, for she is gentle, and she is fragile.

All my love,
Snookie"

He pulled a pencil and a small piece of paper outta his pocket afta starring at dat letter fa awhile and started writing.

"Dear Snookie,

I's feel you, and I see da love in yo eyes. But rite now I's got to be de man dat I am and respect yo flower like I respect God, my mama and my sista,. I's gon walk you home now. From now on dis hea is our tree, cuz I's love you Snookie and I wanna do dis da rite way.

All my love,
Ben"

At furst I's thankin he didn't want me in dat way. But afta reading his letter ova and ova again, it made me fall mo in love wit'em.

Auntee Johnnie Mae won't on de poach when us got there, so dat mean she wuz sleepin. She still ain't met Ben yet, cause lately she already sleep when us git hea. *"You sho dis is whut you want Snookie?"* **He asked wit care in his heart.** *"I's been wantin it fa a long time now Ben, and I's tied of waiting. I understood whut you sayin bout de Lawd, yo sistah and yo ma, but I ain't git'n no yonga."* **I couldn't help but to let de tears fall, he held me in his arms real tight.** *"Let's plan fa next week. Instead of goin to de meetin place, meet me at dat ole Barn house cross de field from de pond."* **He said witta goodnite peck on my lips.**

I kissed my Auntee as she slept soundly on de sofa chair dat she got from Miss Edgewood fa us dis week. I could tell dat she and Miss Clyde had, had a busy day by de smell of peaches in de air and all de mason jars sittin on de

kitchen counter filled wit peach preserve from de peaches dat I picked.

It rained de whole week. But dat won't gon stop us from goin to de juke joint to nite. Ben drove us home but us didn't talk too much on de way cause Essie and Tillie wuz sittin quiet in de back seat, us jes enjoyed de short ride. He grabbed my hand de moment dey got out de car wit a gentle but firm grip, I layed my head on his arm and breath a deep sigh.

I could see Auntee Johnnie Mae sittin on de poach as us pulled up in de yard. Ben asked me to wait befoe I git out de car. He got out and walked round to my side of de car and opened de door fa me. Fa sum reason I wuz kinda embarrassed on de count of Auntee Johnnie Mae wuz sittin on de poach and I knowed she wuz lookin. We walked up on de poach and I introduced them. *"Ben, dis hea is my Auntee Johnnie Mae. She's been holpin take care of us since my mama and daddy died,"* **I said.** *"Auntee Johnnie Mae dis hea is Ben, but eb-body call'em Big Ben as you can see on de count dat he's a big man.* **I had de biggest grin on my face cause I's glad dey finally met.** *He play de guitar down at de juke joint on Friday nites."* **She sat there wit'er legs and arms crossed.** *"How you?"* **She said to him.** *"I's jes fine mamn, how you?"* **He tipped his hat.** *"I's fine, who yo folks?"* **She asked.** *"I's kin to Mollie, she my daddy's baby sistah,"* **he said.** *"Ben Phillips? You Ben Phillips boy?"* **She asked him.** *"Yes mamn dats my daddy."* **She smiled** *"I know dem, yo ma and me went to school together, dey good folks. How she doin?"* **She asked him.** *"She fine, jes fine, thank you fa askin."* **He said smilin.** *"Say hay to her fa me."* **She said.** *"I be sho I will mamn, it wuz nice meetin you Miss Johnnie Mae,"* **he said as us stepped off de poach.** *"Same hea chile, be careful now,"* **She said** lovingly. *"Okay."* **He said. I walked him back to his car, he asked me to meet'em Saturday stead of Sunday. Dat made me nervous cause Saturday wuz de next day, jes thank, I's gon be a woman soon and I sho hope de Lawd hav sump'n fa my folks to do to keep'em busy.** *"Them Phillips is good folks,"* **My Auntee said as I stepped back up on de poach.** *"Always hav worked hard fa whut dey got. I mean us all worked hard but dey real hard workin folks. You don good baby to git yo self hooked up wit one of dem,"* **she said wit dat ole sly grin.** *"Why thank you Auntee. I's wonderin though, my hips don spread sum. You reckon I need to reduce?"* **I asked her.** *"Naw chile, yo weight jes fine like it is,"* **She said as she throwed one arm up.**

"You ought to see him when he up on dat stage playin dat guitar Auntee." **I said as I got up from my chair to sho her how Ben be ackin.**

"*Ooooo wee, honey chile he ain't nuthin but de truth when he play!*" **I said while I's pranced round de poach, she laughed.** "*And then when de crowd git real loud, he'll come off dat there stage and walk round de room jesta playin and dancin and ackin up, dey lov'em too. I's sho wish you could come and see him play jes one time.*" **Ever time I's talkin bout Big Ben I's git all sturd up.** "*And dis hea is how he end it all.*" **I stood on top of de chair and danced while pretendin dat I's playin a guitar.** "*Look at dat gal go, Snookie I didn't know you dance. You betta git down befoe you fall.*" **My Auntee said to me. Miss Vannie from Mosley Street wuz takin her daily walk wit de dogs.** "*Hay Johnnie Mae, how you be?*" **She hollered out.** "*Hay there Miss Vannie, I's be jes fine how you?*" **My Auntee said back.** "*Whut dat gal doin up there!*" **She hollered.** "*Dancin!*" **Said Auntee.** "*You betta git down from there gal befoe you *fall!"* **She hollered again.** *"I don tole her,"* **said Auntee.** *"Okay yall take care now!"* **She walked on down de road wit dem two dogs, sweet lady.**

Chapter 5

De rain wuz comin down hard. Us met at ole man Pennemon's Barn, nobody had used it in years. Ben had a small candle burnin when I got there. I asked him to play sump'n soft fa me, I's loved de way he played dat guitar. Afta he played, he stood up and our eyes locked. Jes like de furst time us met.

He slowly covered my bottom lip wit his full lips, suckin it gently like a piece of candy and then he slowly slipped his tongue in my mouth, it wuz de sweetest thang I's ever tasted. He always kissed me befoe but never like dis. De cologne he wore mixed wit his sweat reminded me of nuthin but a man. He stepped behind me and started kissin me on de back of my neck as he slowly unfasten my blouse. I felt his wome breath on my neck tween

de kisses. He unfasten my skut and everthang fell to de flo. De nite wuz still, wit only de sound of de rain powin down outside. He slid my bra strap down my arm, I's on fie. My flower wuz soaked wit so much moisture till it dampened my panties, it never throbbed like it wuz doin tonite. He whispered in my ear.

"Snookie, you's jes bout as much love as a man like me can want, all wrapped up and delivered to me in a very pretty package, wit so much love and so many kisses all fa me. Yo chocolate skin, so soft and smooth. De scent of yo skin is like a field of flowers whisperin in de wind. Yo eyes sparkle when us together, and I's like de way yo hair cover my chest when you's resting yo head on me, and baby yo lips; I can kiss dem from hea to eternity. I promise you, I's gon be gentle wit yo beautiful flower and I's never do anythang to hurt you, cause I love you girl." **Tears ran down**

my face as he kissed me sum mo. He took his clothes off and held my hands while starring in my eyes. It felt like ever moment wuz movin in slow motion. He wuz a big man but he wuz fit. His stomach wuz neat like bricks on top of one nother and his thighs wuz big and tight, I's couldn't holp but to trimble a lil. *"Dis hea is all of me Snookie, and all of me belong to you."* He tole me wit his heart, I's felt it too. It sked me to be standin there lookin at a man's private parts fa de furst time, cept fa changin my brothas diapers when dey wuz babies. But Big Ben don't wear diapers, and judging by dis long, fat, hard private part of his, I can see why deys call'em "Big Ben."

He grabbed my hand and led me to de pallet dat he fixed up on de flo befoe I's got there. He laid me down and slowly climbed on top of me. I could feel de tip of his manhood jes sittin at de entrance of my flower, it throbbed ever now and then as de moisture from tween my legs wuz wettin it. He gently ran his tongue ova my large chocolate nipples dat wuz now hard as a pencil eraser and sucked dem, real slow. I's magined dat a guitar wuz softly playin in de quiet nite air. He kissed my stomach, my sides, my arms, and my hands. He stuck his tongue in my pushed in belly button, he sucked my fangers, he nibbled my hands gently, my ears and then made his way back to my hard nipples, my body wuz on fie. De candles wuz burnin down, us didn't hav much light left. Us kissed and kissed, and then he kissed my thighs, my knees and then worked his way down to my feet kissin both of'em. And then he covered my big toe wit those full lips of his, it wuz so good. My mind wuz gone cause I won't spectin dis, chile he sucked dat big toe like a baby's pacifie.

It wuz hard at furst when he tempted to enter my flower, he kept his promise though, he wuz gentle. He softly sucked my breast sum mo. My flower, drenched wit juices, squeezed his manhood as he slowly worked it in and out of me. And then he slowly rubbed dis manhood of his gainst my very sensitive flower bud while still gently suckin my breast. Seem like de mo he sucked my nipples, de mo my flower got wet, and befoe I knowed it, sump'n wuz happenin wit my body dat I caint explain, it wuz so good. Tears flowed from my eyes cause I didn't know dat love could feel so good, suddenly his body started shakin. He moaned, and moaned, and moaned, and moaned. Us kissed de whole time de nite dat I's came a woman, I's loved kissin him. Our bodies wuz soaked from sweat, he rested his head on my stomach while I's gently rubbed his sweaty bald head. Afta bout an hour went by of us talkin bout everthang, he tole me dat he wanted to sho me jes how special I wuz to him. He said dat he wanted to taste me. I didn't understand whut he wuz talkin bout. He tole me to jes lay back and enjoy. I's laid back like he tole me to, and honey chile I's did zactly whut he said...I enjoyed my man tastin me.

Big Ben had me ever which-a-way last nite, and now de muscles in my legs sore all ova, I can hardly walk. But most of all my flower is sore, Ben said dats to be expected being dat it wuz my furst time and all. He gon take me to de picture sho in Atlanta next Saturday. I ain't been to Atlanta since I's a lil girl to visit sum kinfolks. I didn't go to church dis moning cause I didn't feel rite goin since I had relations wit out bein married last nite and I's thought dat maybe sumbody would look at me and be able to tell whut I's been doin.

Essie came knockin early dis moning, Sump'n seemed to be ailing her. *"Whut de matter Essie?"* **I asked.** *"Tim took a job in Atlanta and he start a week from now."* **She said wit tears in her eyes.** *"Well ain't you happy fa him?"* **I asked.** *"Dat ain't it Snookie, he want me to* *go wit'em and I jes caint up and leave my friends and family like dat."* **I looked her in de eyes like my Auntee Johnnie Mae would do me.**

"Essie, you can always make new friends. Sides, I's always be hea fa ya." **She laid her head on my shoulder and wiped her eyes wit her fangers.** *"Dat ain't all, I's gon hav a baby and I wanna be hea in Culloden wit my mama when dis hea baby come."* **She whinned, I won't shocked to hea her news bout de baby cause she and Tim been seeing one nother fa a long time now.** *"Well, I guess I's gon be a God mama."* **Us smiled at one nother**. *"How far long is you?"* **She touched her stomach and smiled.** *"Foe months."*

Essie always been a skinny gal. I's thinkin she wuz ever bit of two or three months, dis baby gon be hea foe you know it. *"Oh* *well, while us tellin secrets, I's got sump'n to tell you."* **I wuz quiet fa a minute and then I tole her.** *I's a woman now."* **She held her head up and looked me in de eyes wit her eyes wide open.** *"Ooooo weee Snookie, I bet you won't even gon tell me if I hadn't tole you bout de baby, won't you?"* **I jes smiled at her.** *"Now Essie don't be like dat, you know I's gon tell you sump'n like dat."* **She smiled.** *"Well how wuz it?"* **She ask me, now I's bout to cry.** *"Oh Essie, it wuz so pretty, he wuz so gentle wit me. I's love him so much, and if it wuz him leavin I's follow him anywhere in dis hea world"* **I said.**

"But whut about de Winter Western Festival week and de big celebration dat Mollie is havin at de Juke Joint on Valentine's nite?" **She asked.** *"Dat ain't til six or seven months from hea Essie, you can still come back fa dat, if not fa de whole celebration at least fa Valentine nite at Mollie's."* **I said.** *"I guess so,"* **she said.**

As soon as Tim found a place fa he and Essie to live, my friend wuz gone to Atlanta. Essie wrote me at least twice a week talkin bout how tall sum of de buildings wuz up there and how everthang wuz faster than in Culloden. She say dey stay in a place called South Atlanta in whut dey call a duplex house. Say de folks next door to her love on one nother all night and fight all day. (Essie's voice), *"Dey's got cats all ova de place Snookie and I caint stand it, I wanna come home."* Po Essie, dem cats hangin round like dey do cause she pregnant and dey smellin de milk in her tiddies.

Chapter 6

De rain started to pour down as I's walkin down Sanders Lane from Uncle T's Corner sto. By de time I got to de house, I could see de chullins grabbin de clothes off de line. Auntee Johnnie Mae stood holdin de door open fa dem. De screen on de door wuz all raggedy now wit cotton balls stuck in de small holes to keep de flies and mosquitos from gittin in. I's got to remember to ask Ben to fix it fa me. I's ran de rest of de short way cause lightnin flashed cross de sky. I's love de rain but lightnin I's jes caint git use to.

Auntee Johnnie Mae and me did de regular routine of feedin de yonguns, puttin dem to bed and finding a spot on de poach dat won't wet. Afta while Flo stepped out de door wit a worried look on her face. *"Flo, whut de matter?"*

I asked her. *"I's gotta cut and it won't stop bleedin,"* **she said. Auntee Johnnie Mae grabbed her arm and pulled her close to her, lookin ova her body.** *"I don't see no blood, where you cut at?"* **She asked her.** *"I's cut on my private part Auntee."* **She said wit a whinning tone in her voice dat worried us.** *"Hush now and listen to me, anybody been messin wit you?"* **I asked her.** *"No Snookie, it started dis moning and it messed up my bed sheets too,"* **she cried. De look of relief went cross me and my Auntee's face cause us knowed jes whut it wuz then.** *"My stomach ailing me and I's gotta headache,"* **she said. I grabbed her and wrapped my arms round her tight.** *"OOOhh, baby gurl. You's a young lady now, and eeever month round dis time, God is gon remind you by brangin dis on, it's called yo period. You's jes gon hav to lay down till you feel betta."* **Auntee Johnnie Mae got up from her chair.** *"I's* *gon fix you sum wome tea baby, it's gon be all rite. I's crazy outta my mind when mine started years ago. Us didn't hav de pads back then, so us had to make do wit old rags and all,"* **she said. I stood up and took her by de hand.** *"Come on wit me, let me sho you whut to do."* **I ran her sum wome wawter, gav her sum pads and sum clean nite clothes, and then us sat back out on de poach and talked.** *"Now when dis is goin on wit you, you caint wear no white clothes, nuthin lite colored. You's gon hav sum accidents sumtimes, jes be careful,"* **I tole her.** *"Whut kinda accidents?"* **She asked me.** *"Sumtimes you mite jes be sittin in a chair or sump'n and when you git up, it mite be a red spot on de chair or wherever you wuz sittin,"* **I tole her.**

"Jes try to change dem pads as much as you can, pending on how heavy it's comin," **Auntee tole her, Po chile wuz so sked, she bust in tears. If I's knowed she wuz gon start dis**

early, I'da tole her long time ago. *"I don't like dis,"* **she cried.** *"Well its hea and it ain't goin no where soon. Dis hea is jesta sign from God to let you know dat you can bear yo own chilren when de time is rite. You'll git use to it baby, its gon be all rite,"* **Auntee said.** *"I noticed how yo body been fillin out too, won't be long befoe boys start lookin at you and wantin to come sniffin round hea."* **I tole her.** *"Hea, put yo feet up and relax baby,"* **Auntee tole her as she grabbed her ankles and layed dem in her lap. I held her in my arms and us talked til she fell off to sleep.**

Chapter 7

Ben and me saw one nother mo than ever now. He took me to nice restaurants in Forsyth. But most of de time I's jes wanna go to Mary's Kontry Kitchen, de only fancy restaurant hea in town ret now but dey put'n another one up. Sumtimes on

Fridays now afta de sho us go to Annie Maude's Boarding House to rent a room fa a nite. Annie Maude is a short and skinny feisty woman dat don't take no mess. You can tell she got sum Indian in her blood by her smooth honey color, her pretty soft white hair and dat not so big nose. Breakfast come wit de room and she sho can cook. One time when us got in our special room, Ben had bought me de prettiest sunflowers and daisies from Bell's Flower Shop and had dem sittin ret pretty in a vase on de antique cheery dresser. I's felt like God had dropped a blessin ret in my lap cause of de good ways dat Ben treated me, us take long walks at Alfred Park holdin hands. Sumtimes he stop and kiss me jes cause us still spend our Sunday afta noons at de pond unda our tree. Don't matter how de weather wuz, it wuz jesta wonderful place to be together. He gotta new job at Benny's Lumber Yard ova in Barnesville makin a heep of money. He buys me a new dress once a month from Louise's Dress Shop, and a pair of shoes from Lil Rich Shoe Department ova in Forsyth. Sumtimes I feel bad cause I don't spend much time at home no mo wit my siblings, but Auntee Johnnie Mae said dat I needed to enjoy my life. Say she want me to hav chullins of my own sum day. She thought dat if I raised my siblings wit out havin a life of my own, I probably won't want no chullins of my own if I's ever got married. So ever afta noon Auntee Domp would come ova and holp her wit de chullins. Ebbody called her Auntee cause she pratically raised all of us wit her huneds of switches dat stood up tall in a bucket on her poach. Mama always said if you wanna train a chile rite, stang'em witta switch.

Tillie came ova dis evening, us sat out on de poach sheddin peas. She tole me dat she seen Ben ova in Macon wit another woman. I tole her dat it wuz probably jes sumbody who wuz sum kin to him. Wonda why she tellin me dis, I thought to myself. She knows how me and Ben feel bout one nother. *"Tillie, Ben and me too close to mess up whut us got goin,"* **I tole her. She stared at me in a way like she felt sorry fa me.** *"I know Snookie, but I's yo friend and I's love ya. And I's fugure you ought to hea dis from a friend foe anybody else brang it to ya,"* **she said.** *"Tillie whut you talkin bout?"* **I asked.** *"Snookie, de gurl wuz big and dey wuz holdin hands."* **At dat moment I's felt like sumbody had hit me on de head witta hamma. Tears weld up in my eyes as I starred at Tillie.** *"Well I's sho there's a reason fa dat Tillie, no use in jumpin to all kinds of clusions* *ova it."* **Who wuz I foolin? Dis news wuz taring me up on de inside sump'n bad.** *"Baby, it don't git no clearer than whut I saw, now I's know dis hea is hard fa ya to bear ret now. I's gon head on home so you can hav sum time to ya self to clear ya mind."* **She got up and left, leavin me sittin there stuck wit de thoughts dat she had jes put in my spirit bout my man. Tillie always hav been de jealous type, keepin up mess in eb-body's relations. She jes mad cause**

none of dem band members want her. No matter how she prance round dat room wit'er ole dried up self tryin to git dey tention. Us put up wit'er cause us always felt sorry fa her. Now she buttin in my bizness and I ain't gon hav it. She been in dat house by herself fa so long, she don got herself miserable and she want eb-body else to be miserable ret long wit'er. I's gon

go ret ova to Ben's ret now and nip dis in de bud. I called fa Flo to finish sheddin de peas and then I headed to Ben's house. I thought to myself as I wuz on my way to Ben's. Whut if dis is true whut Tillie said? How would I handle it, would I lose my mind? Whut if de gurl is at his house ret now? I's sked now cause I don't know whut to expect when I's git hea. well it's too late now cause I's standing at de door.
I's beatin on dat door foe I's knowed it, and hard too. Ben

finally opened it standin there wearin nuthin but a pair of pants. *"Hey baby, whut you knockin so hard fa?"* He asked. And I jes got straight to bizness, cause by now I's cryin. *"Tillie tole me dat she saw you in Macon wit sum pregnant woman holdin hands!"* He wrapped his big arms round me and walked me inside and sat me down at de table. *"Snookie, you know I's never do a thang to hurt you gurl, whut us got is fa real."* **He said.** *"Well how come she tole me dat tale Ben? She made it sound true to me,"* **I wuz still cryin. He pulled me ova to him and sat me in his lap**. *"Baby, dat woman wuz my sistah, member Bay-Sis? I tole you bout'er when us furst sat unda dat tree."* **I didn't believe him, I wuz taring up on de inside cause I thought he wuz tellin a tale.** *"Matta fact, I introduced dem to one nother, why she tole you dat mess, I don't know,"* **he said and by dat time I heard a car pull up in de yard and a minute later a pretty dark skinned pregnant girl walked in de door witta man toting her bags.** *"Nola, dis hea is my gurl, Snookie."* **Ben said smilin de way I's smilin de furst time he met my Auntee. She came ova to me and gav me a tight hug.** *"Hay Snookie!"* **She said in her squeaky high pitched voice.** *"Ben don tole me so much bout you, I's feels like I's* *knowed you fa years! Dis hea is my husband Walt, us live ova in Macon. I ain't seen Ben since last year so us cided to surpris'em yesterdi and then us all went shoppin ova in Macon."* **I's feelin bad fa even believin dat ole Tillie.**

"De gurl us saw at de sto yesterday tole Snookie dat I had got a woman pregnant. So she came ova hea ta beat me up." **He said smilin, I's pop'em on de hand.** *"Stop dat Ben, I's already embarrass enough."* **I really wuz shame of myself.** *"Chile please, you ain't got nuthin to worry yo pretty face bout cause Ben loves you. Sumtime you hav to keep eye on yo so called friends."* **She wuz rite, cause sumtime Tillie say thangs to git next to people on purpose. It's like she git sum kinda good feelin from dat jesta make herself feel betta or powerful. And de sad part bout it is dat she thank don't nobody know it. I's member one time**

she bought her cousin from Hampton to de Juke Joint. Her cousin wuz a real nice gurl but afta she left, Tillie tole me dis tale bout seein Ben watchin her cousin as if he wanted her. I tole her dat I ain't got no hold on Ben, if he want her cousin then he could hav'er. De thang dat got to me wuz dat I couldn't believe dat she sit up and jes thank of thangs of de devil. I's gon invite her to suppa afta church. Ben gon be there too and I's gon see how she ack then. Nola and Walt left to go git sump'n to eat fa suppa.

Ben sat there wit me still on his lap staring into my eyes. He turned my body towards his and strapped my legs round his body. I's wearin a long dress, so naturally I felt him de moment he pulled me to his body. He unzipped his pants and pulled his thang out. And then he ripped de seam of my panties and rubbed gainst me. It didn't take much fa me to git sturd up cause by now Ben knowed jes which tiddie to put in his mouth to git me started. I's hotter than a peppa sittin in de sun and my flower wuz filled wit juices. He slipped it in slowly, I straddled my legs round his body in dat chair tighter as I moved my body up and down on him. I gripped his thang tight as I's squeezin my flower muscles ever single time I's lifted up off of'em. Silence filled de air wit jes us breathin and moanin hard. De mo he sucked my tiddies, de hotter I got and de mo us both moaned. *"Sorry fa thankin dat you won't bein honest wit me,"* **I cried to him.** *"I's love you baby, I tole you dat I ain't goin no where,"* **he said. And at dat moment my body burst to dat good feelin wit my juices rushin out, drownin his thang. Us did it two mo times befoe he walked** me home, I don't thank I's ever git enough of'em.

Chapter 8

Auntee Johnnie Mae gav me a nice pair of paink shoes. I wore dem to church wit de nice paink dress dat Ben bought me awhile back. De choir wuz sangin, "I Am De Way." De vibration of de music unda my feet ret long wit de foot stompin on dem hardwood floors and de sounds of dem tambourines all ova dat church wuz startin to move me. Hanna fell out furst and then I seen furst lady hoopin and hollin, and befoe I's knowed it I's jumpin up and down in de spirit too, screamin hallaluhahs and thank you Jesus all ova de place.

I could hea Flo's voice as de music slowed down sangin, "Precious Memories." Dat chile know she can sang, Lawda mussy! It won't a dry eye in de place when she sang dat song. Auntee Johnnie Mae wuz pacing de floor wit both hands up praisin de Lawd screamin, *"Sang it chile, Thank you Jesus!"* Fa Flo to be as young as she is, she had a sangin voice like an ole soul. Reverend Ivey preached a good sermon today too, I mean he walked dat word honee chile and he said it when he said it.

Us all changed outta our church clothes soon as us got to de house. Flo set de table while me and Auntee Johnnie Mae womed de food up. I cut de cone bread up in squares, ran wawter ova them and then put'em in de oven all wrapped in foil. Us went on and made de cone bread cause us knowed company wuz comin afta church. Reverend Ivey and his family came by to eat wit us too. Reverend Ivey is a tall dark man, but he good lookin. He gotta pretty dark skinned wife and chullin too, I think his son is sweet on Flo. I's knowed dey be comin round sniffin sooner or later.

"Reverend Ivey, you sho preached dat word today brotha," **said Auntee.** *"Why thank you sistah,"* **he said back.** *"Yeeessss, and you said it when you said it,"* **she said.** *"Yea he did,"* **I agreed. By de time everthang wuz ready, Tillie knocked at de door, she didn't know dat Ben wuz gon be hea. I smelled alcohol on her breath, I always knowed she carried dat bottle in her pocketbook to church, jes devilish. She gon bust hell wide open. She sat at my suppa table wit me, my man and my siblings and ack like she never tole me bout Ben and Nola.** *"Baby you looked so sweet dis moning all sugared down in yo paink at church."* **Ben said to me from cross de table, my panties got wet from de way dem words rolled off his tongue. My man know he gotta way wit words.**

"Thank you baby," **I said.** *"Aawwwww, praise de Lawd. I do believe it won't be long befoe us hav a wedding sistah Johnnie Mae,"* **said the Reverend.**

Tillie didn't hav much food at her house so I fixed her a plate to take wit'er fa later. Ben walked her to de poach, and when he came back inside he tole me how she wuz tryin to git'em to drive her home cause she won't feelin good. Then he say she jes came ret out and tole him dat she wuz lonely and wanted his company later tonite. *"She be all rite,"* **I tole him in my sweet voice. Minutes afta dat us saw de Reverend and his family off and then us sat on de poach wit Auntee Johnnie Mae and talked fa awhile.**

Ben finally left and I couldn't wait to git to Tillie's house two blocks ova. I's cut ret cross Miss

Donna's yard to git there faster, she finally opened da door afta I knocked fa awhile. She stood there witta ole smurk on her face, wearin big paink hair rollers. Tillie wuz bout a few inches shorter than me, her skin complexion wuz a pale yella. Grandma used to call it "Ole shit color." *"Hay gurl, I's jes thankin bout how nice it wuz of you to giv me a plate to brang home wit me."* **She said all happy.** *"Tillie, I's jes gon cut ret to de chase hea, I invite you to my home and I feed you cause I's thankin you my friend, and then you stand in front of my house and try to coast my man to comin to yo house cause you say you lonely, if you lonely honey git a dog or cat. Most folks don't want nuthin to do witcha cause of yo ways. I still talk to you but you ain't welcome to my house no mo. And dis hea ain't bout no man, its bout respect."* **She stared at me wit dem red drunken eyes of hers.** *"Caint we jes share him Snookie?"* **I**

couldn't believe whut dis heffa jes said to me. *"Tillie, I hope you choke on dat food, don't come round me no mo cause sump'n jes ain't rite witcha!"* **I left and I felt ret good bout tellin her off.**

Chapter 9

Fall came and went, so did Thanksgiving. Ben and sum of de other men had a hard time tryin to catch dem turkeys. He gav me a nice red sweater fa Christmas and he stayed ova on Christmas Eve to put de boys wheels together. He made Auntee Johnnie Mae sit down and put'er feet up since she wuz always holpin out round de house. Us cooked everthang cept fa de red velvet cake, my Auntee made de best red velvet cakes and custard pies. Ever time one thang wuz done us take my Auntee a sample of it. She finally drifted off on a full stomach from all dat food testing.

Us finished gatherin de chullins toys and clothes and sat dem in separate places witta Christmas stockin dat had each one of dey names on it, and then us tipped in my bedroom. He said he wuz jes gon lay wit me til I fall off to sleep and he wuz gon wait fa me in de kitchen. Us didn't want nobody to wake up and catch'em in my bed, specially Auntee Johnnie Mae. I took a quick shower and climbed in my bed where I do most of my thinkin bout'em at, and ret in his arms. He slipped unda de covers and befoe I's knowed it...he wuz tastin me. He ain't did dat since de furst nite but you know me...I's laid back and quietly enjoyed my man tastin me, ooooo chile. I whispered fa him to stop when I felt de good feelin comin. I guess he didn't hea me, I's tried pushin his head away but he grabbed my hands and held'em down and kept doin it, I wanted to scream. I manage to pry one hand from his tight grip and grabbed a pilla to cover my face as I let out de loudest scream of pleasure while my body gav way to de good feelin, he wuz lost in it. He got up and went in de bathroom, I waited fa him to come back but he didn't.

I's sleepin like a baby, only to wake up to de sounds of happy screams from de chullins. I went in de kitchen afta washin my hands and face to find Ben sittin up in de chair sound asleep. I's rubbed his shoulders and kissed him on de neck and whispered, *"I's love you"* in his ear and then sent him to my room to lay down, I stood in de doorway watchin de chullins play. *"Go wash yall hands and face and come on in hea and eat you sum poast toast, and pic dis room up a lil so it won't git too junky."* I said to dem. *"Okay!"*

Dey all said at de same time, each one of'em gav me a big hug as dey headed to de bathroom.

"Where's Auntee Johnnie Mae?" **I asked my nine year ole sistah Lilah Mae.** *"She had to go git sump'n from her house, she say she be ret back."* **She tole me, my lil brotha Willie Lee wuz walkin witta limp as he came from de bathroom.** *"Whuts ailing you Will Lee?"* **I asked him.** *"I fell ova dat dare toy."* **He answered.** *"Go git de bucket and fill it wit sum hot water, hot as you can stand it and put a lil epson salt in it and soak it fa awhile, you'll be all rite afta while."* **Lilah Mae walked up to me.** *"Snookie, can us go outside?"* **I looked down at her wit my hands on my hips.** *"Yeah, put sum wome clothes on, and yall betta not be out there chunkin no rocks, ya hea?"* **She smiled as she ran to de bedroom to put on sum clothes.** *"Yeees!* **She screamed back. By dat time Auntee Johnnie Mae wuz comin in de door wit presents in her arm.** *"Snookie, I dreamed about fish all nite long, you big gal?"* **She asked.**

"Now Auntee Johnnie Mae, why you ask me a fool thang like dat fa?" **I tried to sound innocent.** *Cause I know dat you and Ben been havin relations wit one nother...and often...I ain't no fool."* **I tried to convince her dat she wuz all wrong.** *"Auntee dats all in yo head, Ben and me ain't doin a thang."* **I said.** *"Don't sprute my word gal, I ain't no fool, I see de change in you."* **Us stood there starring at one nother, then us both jes let out de biggest laugh.** *"I gav de chullins sum poast toast jes to put sump'n on dey stomach befoe breakfast,"* **I tole her as us started to prepare our big Christmas breakfast. She put de radio on de gospel station. I sat at de ole round wooded table and watched her dance a holy dance as she stirred the cheese in de grits. She yelled out** *"Yeeeeaaah, thank you Jesus!"* **wit one hand up praisin de Lawd ever now and then. It wuz gittin late so I cided to wake Ben up.**

"Ima wake Ben up," **She snapped at me.** *"Leav'em be, let'em sleep till everthang is done."* **She said hastly, and then she suddenly remembered dat de bread wuz at de bottom of de oven.** *"Snookie, take de bread out. Make ace befoe it burn up, oh God I forgot all about it!"* **She said, but it wuz jes rite.**

Flo got a job babysittin on de weekends fa Lulu and her husband. Dey had a pretty lil high yella baby gurl named Kali. Dat baby cried de furst two times her ma bought her hea. But I's ready fa her de third time. I had sum peanut butter on a spoon waitin fa her, babies love peanut butter on a spoon.

Essie came back wit her new baby a month early. She had a gurl too, pretty lil chocolate thang she called Naki, African name dat means furst bone female chile. *"Dats a pretty name Essie,"* I said as she changed de baby's diaper and wiped de chile's face wit it. Dey say if you wash a baby's face wit it's pissy diaper, it'll make dey skin smooth and pretty, us been doin it fa years wit new babies round hea. Lil Naki had a bad cold and wuz all congested, Miss Doris blew her nose cause Essie couldn't brang herself to do it. She laid her in her lap face up, gently pressed down on one of de baby's nostril and blew through de otha one wit'er mouth and befoe us knowed it, snot wuz ever where. *"Essie you need to shape dis baby's head so it won't be all outta shape when she grows up,"* Said Miss Doris. I's grabbed de baby from her and started rubbin her head round and round. Miss Doris went in de kitchen to fix up sump'n fa de baby's chest cause it wuz still full of cold. She took an ole sheet and tore it up in pieces. And then she put a piece of it in a fryin pan and sturd sum olive oil, a lil flour and sum onions in it. She wrapped de onions up in dat cloth and then tied it up wit another piece of cloth long enough to wrap round de baby's waist. She sat de part dat had de onions in it on de baby's navel

and then tied it up good on de baby.

It had a awful smell to it but us knowed by moning she wuz gon be breathin betta. *"Essie, Auntee Johnnie Mae tole me to tell you not to bite yo baby's nails."* **I said to her.** *"Why not?"* **She asked me.** *"She say it'll make her grow up to be rogish,"* **I tole her.** *"Oh chile please,"* **she said. Miss Doris walked in de room dryin her hands off wit a kitchen towel.** *"You betta listen chile cause I don't want my lil sweet sugah to grow up steeling."* **She said as she kissed de baby's hand.** *"And jes so you'll know, if dis hea baby git constipated, don't go runnin to no doctor. Jes take a lil piece of soap and stick it up her butt and foe you know it, she'll be runnin off all ova de place. Dats how us black folk been survivin all these years in these hea back woods, God don blessed us wit common sense."* **She said, and she wuz rite.**

Essie and de baby stayed a few mo days and then my friend wuz gone back to Atlanta. She wuz good and use to de city now cause dey moved to a betta neighborhood. She say Atlanta got all kinda jobs dat pay a heep of money, say dey got rich coloreds up there too.

Chapter 10

De five day winter fest wuz finally hea. folks from all ova came dis year on de count of de band. Did I ever tell you de name of Ben's band? Hot Butta Biscuits and syrup is whut deys call, cause deys hot like butta covered biscuits all sopped up wit sum smooth syrup! Ben got a cousin dat came ova from Nawleans. His name be Ray and he play de saxophone, he good but us use to a lot of sangin in these hea back woods. Ray had smooth chocolate skin, teeth white as egg whites, and a nice clean cut beard. He kinda on de thick side but it looks good on him, and he wore his cap tipped on his head.

I made a dress for each day. Essie's mama, Ms. Doris holped me wit de hems and all. I even let my hair down fa de occassion,

Ben loves my long deep wavy black hair.

Two bands played each nite. Honey, dat Juke Joint wuz filled wit heeps of peeple comin from all ova, but us made sho us got there early to git a good table. Even old Miss Rooty showed her face once or twice. I don't even know her real name, eb-body gav her dat name on de count of her messin round wit roots wit ole Mae Lee and all. Deys been de towns root workers foe I's even bone. Mollie cided to giv a prize to de best band at de end of de festival.

Essie came dat Saturday nite, she de prettiest mama I's ever seen. I won't sho if she wuz gon come cause she been so busy wit de baby, I sho don't want her to go back to Atlanta, us hugged one nother tight. *"Gurl I wuz crazy to tell you to go to Atlanta, caint he jes live hea in Culloden and travel to work from hea?"* **I asked her in my whining voice.** *"I don't know Snookie, but I do know dat I wanna be ret hea in Culloden wit all my friends, specially you."* **Us stood there smilin at one nother.** *"I's jes tied of not havin a real friend like you round, Tillie up to her ole ways again, so I had to turn her loose."* **At dat very moment I felt a big splash of wawter hit my back. It coulda been beer, who knows? All I's know is dat it wuz cold and my back wuz soak and wet.** *"Snookie, you got sump'n to say bout me, you say it to my face!"* **Tillie screamed at me.** *"Tillie, is you crazy!"* **I screamed back, I wuz so mad at her fa wettin me up like dat. I had no earthly idea dat she had came wit Essie, I guess she hadn't tole Essie dat us won't speakin no mo.** *"You thank you sump'n witcho ole ugly rags and all, he gon dump you jes wait and see!"* **She wuz drunk as usual, Essie**

stepped tween us facing Tillie. *"Tillie, honey chile whut is de matter wit you, why you acking like dis!"* **She asked her. I stepped in front of Essie and stood close to Tillie's face, I could smell de liquor on her breath.** *"I ain't gon make no fool outta myself bout a man in hea Tillie, so you best to jes git on way from me befoe I's giv it to ya like yo ma shoulda did long time ago."* **I wuz still burnin mad wit dat gal.** *"No, I'll giv it to you like yo mama oughta now!"* **she said confusing me a lil bit but I jes blamed it on her drunkness.** *"Tillie I swear, you speak gainst my dead mama one mo time I's gon git cha, now I'ma put dis past me and I's gon walk away now like a real woman pose to do."* **She put'er hands on her hips and stepped in my face.** *"Honey use de five senses de Lawd don gav yah, ebbody know dat yo dead mama wuz really yo Auntee, and yo Auntee Johnnie Mae is yo real mama. She wuz ho hoppin all ova town and she* *got knocked up wit you by a band member and,"* **I slapped her to de flo befoe I's knowed it, and us fightin like two alley cats, I don't even know who pulled us part from one nother. All I's member is bein in de car cryin and screamin all de way home, Essie wuz sho she never hurd such a tall tale. Wonda where Tillie hea a fool tale like dat from? I's wondering and shakin all ova.**

I stepped in de house wit my dress ripped and my hair wuz messy from de fight. Auntee Johnnie Mae jumped up from de sofa chair hollerin. *"Snookie whut's wrong, what happened to ya!"* **She said witta sked look in her face.** *"Me and Tillie had a fist fight."* **I's cryin still cause of whut she had said.** *"Whut on earth fa, where she at, I's sick and tied of dat bald head heffa!"* **I stood there watchin her as she reached behind de brown recliner fa her stick...jes**

like a mama bout to go to battle...fa her chile, never paid it no tention till now. *"Auntee Johnnie Mae, I's gon ask you sump'n...and mo than everthang in dis world I's want you to tell me de truth."* **I said wit tears still runnin down my face.** *"Whut's ailing you chile?"* **She asked witta worried look in her eyes.** *"Is you my mama?."* **I asked wit fear in my heart, she wuz numb. She sat down slowly onto de recliner chair starring in space.** *"Where you hea dat from Snookie?"* **She asked me in a deep low voice like sumbody had jes hit'er in de stomach.** *"Tillie stood in de Juke Joint and nounced it all proud and mighty to eb-body."* **She sat quiet a few minutes longer, still starring in de air and then she started to talk.** *"Me and Miller met when us wuz jes leven years ole, us played in de creek everday collecting tad poles and keepin eye on dem til dey turn to frogs and then us send'em off like* deys our own chilrens. Us caught bumble bees, lightin bugs, butta flies, everthang. By de time us got to be thirteen, us madly in love wit one nother. Nothin or nobody could keep us part from de other. **She stopped talkin fa a minute and then she started to speak again.** "Us foolin round one day at dat creek, neither one of us knowed a thang bout sex, us jes stumbled up on it one day I guess you can say. So in our young minds afta dat furst time, us wuz already married since us had joined our bodies together as one, never knowed love could go such a distance. Two peeples body parts all ova one nother like dat, it wuz a beautiful thang. Miller took me to a wonderful place ever time us joined tagether as one." **Tears started to fall from her eyes as she kept talkin.** "Next thang I know months down de road, sump'n wuz movin in me. Mama took me to Ms. Rooty's house to do way wit it, she made me take a heep of turpentine to kill it. I's sked, I's so *sked. Cause I always hurd talk dat if you do way witta baby, you'll hea it cryin fa you on yo death bed. And God knows I didn't want to hea a dead baby cryin while I's on my death bed. Anyhow, I's too far long to git rid of it so us had a family meetin and since I wuz jes thirteen, I didn't hav no say in it. My best friend and only sistah wuz nineteen at de time. Eb-body agreed dat she and her boyfriend*

of five years would marry and raise de baby as theirs. Miller's folks sent him up nawth to live wit sum kin folks and us never saw one nother again. I thought to myself dat dis too shall past, and then I vowed dat I's never be wit another man cause otha than God, Miller wuz my everthang. I thought about bein wit sumbody else jes to git Miller off my mind when he wuz gone, but I jes couldn't brang myself to do it cause evertime I looked in yo eyes I saw Miller's, and it reminded me of de love me and him had." De only thang dat I had to hold on to dat wuz part of him and me dey took from me and forced me to go on all these years callin you my niece. I wanted you to know who yo folks wuz but I wuz young and mama woulda beat me if I said one word. Knowin dat I could be by yo side everday of yo life eased de pain, cause I's giv my life fa you Snookie. Yo nickname is de only thang dey let me be part of. But whut dey didn't know is dat Snookie wuz whut me and Miller called one nother. Dats why I's know you so good. You and Ben got a love jes like de love yo daddy and me had. I figure I's take care of my sistahs chilren and giv my baby de chance dat I couldn't git at true love. I's sorry you had to find out de way you did, but everthang happen fa a reason. I guess she had to tell ya so I could be set free from de truth. I hope you can find it in yo heart to forgiv me sumday." **I's knowed xactly whut she wuz feelin. She stood up to leave de** room, I grabbed her by de hand. *"I forgav you de moment she tole me, mama."* Us held one nother harder than us ever did befoe fa a long time, I looked her in de eyes. *"Whut dat ole devil Tillie meant fa evil, turned out to be fa de gooood."* I tole her. *"I's love you baby."* She tole me. *"And I's love you back."* I tole her.

Ben came by to see if I wuz all rite. I tole him everthang, and then I tole him dat I won't goin to de festival finale de next nite. He said dat I had to come cause he caint play rite if he caint see my face sittin in de front where I always been. So I cided dat I wuz gon go, he said dat Mollie tole Tillie to never come to her place of bizness no mo. I fell asleep in his arms thankin bout de pain dat Johnnie Mae had been through these past twenty five years, God bless her.

Us sat on de poach afta breakfast and talked as usual, it wuz like sum where deep inside of me I always knowed dat it wuz sump'n bout de bond us had, now I know. She cided to go to church wit out de chullins dis moning, she needed dat time to herself. I sat in a hot tub of wawter wit sum Epson Salt on de count of my muscles bein sore from de fight. Us had neckbones, turnip greens, macaroni and cheese wit cone bread muffins fa suppa. Auntee Johnnie Mae cooked an apple pie.

Us cided dat round de chullins she wuz Auntee so dey don't git confused. Us et sum Mayfield homemade vanilla ice cream wit dat pie. And then I took a two hour nap so I could look fresh fa de festival finale tonite.

I stepped proudly in de doorway of de Juke Joint one hour early wearin my long ruffled red western dress wit brown trimmings that showed a lil bosom, Essie got up from her chair to greet me wit a hug. *"I's so glad you came tonite Snookie,"* **she tole me.** *"Essie, Tillie wuz rite bout my Auntie bein my real mama, cept fa my daddy didn't play in no band." Dey wuz thirteen, his folks sent him away to live up nawth and then dey moved and haven't been hurd of since. It don't make me feel no different fa her, I's love her even mo than ever, us happy."* **I explained to her.** *"Well praise de Lawd,"* **She said raisin her hand in de air.**

Ben's band finally had de stage afta foe other bands had played, but Ben won't on stage. I started to git worried til sumbody opened de double barn doors to de left of us, the chill from de

cold weather came in de room. And whut I saw next wuz sump'n I won't expectin, I don't thank no body wuz expectin it. Ben wuz sittin on top of his horse wearin a tan western outfit wit boots and a hat to match, and he wuz playin dat guitar like never befoe. He guided de horse to our table and jumped down off of it and walked ova to me and grabbed my hands. A chair wuz sittin on de stage. He guided me to de chair and sat me down and got down on one knee and then opened up a pretty box dat had a beautiful ring in it. De room wuz so quiet you could hea a rat pissin on cotton, he grabbed de microphone and put it up to his mouth. *"Snookie, eb-body in town knows how much I's love you. I wanna be wit you fa de rest of my life...will you be my wife?"* I couldn't stop cryin. *"Yes, yes!"* I screamed, everbody wuz clappin, hollerin, and whistlin.

Essie wuz cryin too, she my best friend, she grabbed my hand when I got back to de table.

Smoked filled de doorway of de double doors and Ben's cousin Ray stepped from behind dat smoke wearin all white wit a long white coat dat went to his ankles. He wuz playin dat saxophone, we finally got use to his music cause sumtime it seemed like dat sax wuz havin a conversation wit you. Tonite, Ray wuz playin one dat he called De Blu Sofa Chair, it wuz pretty. He jes played dat thang and befoe you know it, he don named whatever it is he playin. De women wuz puttin money and everthang in his pockets as he walked round dat room playin dat sax, Ray wuz smooth and had de good looks to go wit it. Afta he did his solo, de band showed out till it wuz ova! Ben tole me dat he'd be by de house

afta dey finished packin up everthang. De kitchen wuz still open so me and Essie ordered a plate of hot fish wit fries and cole slaw. Essie wuz back and forth sayin hay to people she ain't seen since she left.

A strange man sat at our table while Essie wuz still walkin round. *"How you doin miss?"* **He said wit a proper tone as he tipped his hat to me.** *"I's fine, dis seat is takin."* **I tole him.** *"I know, I was just curious to know where you get the name Snookie from,"* **he said.** *"My mama gav me dat name, but my real name is Sabrina. Why you ask?"* **I said. He starred at me for a minute or two wit out sayin a word.** *"I lived here twenty-five years ago. I'm stayin ova at Annie Maude's Boarding House while I take care of some business here."* *I was hoping to run into my best friend while I'm here but I'm not sure if she's still here or if I would even recognize* *her, hell I don't even know if she's still alive."*

Wait a minute, I's thankin to myself. Dis couldn't be, he say he left dis town twenty-five years ago and his best friend is a she. By dis time my hands wuz shakin. I looked back up at'em. *"Are you okay?"* **He asked me witta smooth nawthern tone, Johnnie Mae did say dat his folks sent him up nawth. All of a sudden I wuz lookin at myself from cross dat table, I's lookin jes like dis man. Dey say I's born witta veil ova my face, which made me extra special cause I picked up on thangs faster than others. Johnnie Mae jes said last nite dat thangs happen fa a reason, he kept on talkin.** *"Now back to your name."* **I cut'em off.** *"It's a long story, a long love story...Miller."* **I couldn't hold it, my eyes wuz filled up wit tears.** *"I instantly felt her spirit when the guitar player said* *your name, I couldn't let you leave without me asking you."* **I could see de tears weldin up in his eyes.** *"Twenty-five years, I always wondered about you two. I've never found love the way I found it with a pretty cookie years ago named Johnnie Mae. Tell me daughter, how is she?"* **He asked as he grabbed my hands and squeezed dem tight.** *"You ain't gon believe dis, but I jes found out who I wuz last nite. She fine, she cried fa you last nite."* **At dat point he buried his face in my hands and wept like no man I know had ever wepted befoe, it drew de tention of Ben so he came ova to see whut de matter wuz.** *"Baby, dis hea is my daddy."* **I wuz cryin again.**

Us pulled up in de yard wit Miller in his car behind us. I asked him to giv me a minute to prepare my mama, I sat next to her on de poach, she could tell I had been cryin again. *"Whut's wrong now chile?"* **She asked so lovingly.** *"A miracle happened tonite at Mollie's. Furst, Ben asked me in front of eb-body to marry him. And member last nite when you said dat everthang happen fa a reason?* **I asked.** *"Yes,"* **she answered.** *"Well, I's sittin at my table and dis man who hurd Ben call me Snookie came up to me and asked me where I got de name from."* **I started cryin again.** *"I's gon stop hea and let him tell you de rest."* **I motioned fa Ben to bring my daddy up to de poach and as he rested his foot on de furst step her eyes widened. She let out a scream so loud it made me bust in big blobs of tears. Dey held one nother tight and cried fa de longest, Ben and me stepped off de poach.** *"Us gon* *take a drive so yall can catch up on de lost times."* **I tole dem. Dey wuz lost in one nother, it wuz a beautiful site to see. My real mama and daddy, back to dat wonderful place dat dey shared ova twenty years ago, de Lawd sho work in mysterious ways. Turns out dat Tillie is a distant cousin of my daddy. Ain't dat sump'n? She knowed he wuz comin down home long ago from sum of her other folks who tole her de story dat she got wrong on purpose. She didn't care, long as she figure it wuz hurtin me. Sum people are jes like dat I's reckon, but it's de best thang she don fa me and she don't even know it.**

Ben and me stayed at Maude's so my real mama and daddy could catch up wit one nother. So much had gone on dis week, us both wuz tied. I woke up in de middle of de nite to go out fa a lil air cause Maude musta had de heata on hell as hot as it wuz in dis place. I went out on de poach, it wuz a gread big ole wrap around one too, wit nice furniture from Foot's Furniture Sto. De biggest furniture sto owed by coloreds. He and his two friends, BH and David owned it.

Miss Maude wuz sittin out herself. *"Hay Miss Maude, you all rite?"* **I asked her.** *"Yeah chile, jes restin my feet from moppin de flo,"* **she tole me.** *"Ben asked me to marry him to nite,"* **I tole her.** *"Yeah, I's hurd. I's happy fa yall,"* **she tole me.** *"Thank you,"* **I tole her.** *"Me and my man been married fa a long, long time now,"* **she tole**

me. *"Yall ever git tied of one nother?"* **I asked her.** *"Chile yes, but eb-body go through dat, you jes gotta stay strong. Forgiv a whole heep, love a whole heep, pray a whole heep, laugh a whole heep, and hav a whole heep of patience. And chile when you cookin fa him, take all dat fanger nail polish off. My Jimmy tole me when us furst got married dat I had to take de nail polish off cause it chips, and you never know when it's gon chip off in your food while you's cookin. It made a heep of sense to me, and I's loved him so I didn't wear it no mo. There's gon be times when you jes ain't gon want to giv'em no lovin either, but my vice to you is to jes giv it to him anyhow, no matter how tied you is cause it'll save you a whole heep of fussin wit one nother. And afta you giv'em all dat sweet love, git on up and wash yoself off befoe you fall off to sleep. And if he already don fell to sleep, jes take a wet rag and wash'em off down there, and if he want sum mo in de middle of de nite,* *giv it to him. Ain't nuthin like sum sweet love in de moning befoe startin yo day,"* **she smiled.** *"Tell'em whut you want cause dey don't know. Its up to us to open our mouths to let'em know how we want to feel in de bedroom. Giv'em whut he want, it's all rite long as it ain't sump'n dats gon cause you a heep of pain cause if you don't, a ho will. And another thang when you messin wit a man's food. Honee don't never cook his food while you's still wearin yo nite clothes, put sum clothes on and serve it to him hot. Clean de dishes as you go so you won't hav to do nuthin but wash yown's and his plate afta suppa. Sum of these gals wit husbands and a house full of chullins thank dey can serve dat man his food on a paper plate ret long wit de chullins, don't you do dat. Always giv'em his food on a real plate when you serve it to him, napkin, salt, peppa, tall icy glass of his favorite drank and all, you hea me?"* **I's jes knodded my head while I's takin**

all dis in. I already knowed sum of dis but not all of it, she kept on talkin. *"You see chile, a man works hard and take a heep of mess off folks jes to keep thangs together in his own home. Ben might work hard in de day time, but his love is playin dat guitar, so respect whut he do. And don't git mad if you see another woman in his face ever now and then at dat Juke Joint cause it come wit de territory. Jes know dat its you he love and its you who he goin home wit. Ain't nuthin wrong wit givin him a nice foot bath and a good back rub ever now and then either. Say nice thangs to him like how handsum he is or how much you pree shate him. Buy him sump'n nice ever now and then, cept shoes and watches. Dey say if you buy yah man or woman a pair of shoes, dey'll walk out yo life. And if you buy a watch, dat means de relationship is almost out of time."* **I won't gon believe dat tale bout de shoes and de watch many times Ben don bought me shoes**

from Lil Rich Shoe Department. I jes listen to her cause it wuz de respectful thang to do I's reckon. *"Jes lov'em wit all yo mite, you'll be all rite. But all dis I's tellin you don't mean you gotta take no mess from him either, yah hea?"* **I jes looked at her.** *"Yes mamn, I's hea you and I's thank you fa tellin me all dis."* **She got up to go in de house, she opened de screen door and looked back at me through de screen.** *"And another thang, when you start havin babies fa him. Keep dem chullins clean, don't be let nem walk round all snot nose. And keep plenty of switches round de house cause dem same sweet babies gon grow to be like demon seeds."* **I chuckled while I sat there wit my arms crossed.** *"Yes mamn, I will."* **I tole her.**

(Nine months later)

I's thankin to myself as I's sittin on de screened- in poach of me and Ben's new house how I always wanted a wedding during de cold season, it wuz de second week in November. De leaves on de trees still had de pretty colors on dem. Mama and daddy wuz mo happy than dey wuz when deys chullins. Ben and me got married in de ole school house near de Pennamon's Farm. Everthang wuz yella and white wit gold trimmings, I got dressed at de Pennamon's home.

De school house wuz up de road a lil bit from de house. I stepped on de poach wearin a customed designed dress dat my daddy had ordered from C. Bromfield Company of New Yalk, he paid fa everthang! De invitations nouncements from Hooks Printing is sump'n I's gon keep forever. Us pree shated eb-body closin down dey bizness jes to come to de wedding. Even ole Doc Barnard closed down his pharmacy. Since all de band members wuz in de wedding, one of de bands from de festival played fa us as a gift, The T. Elder Trio played so pretty. My daddy had a man dat went by de name of jes E to come and sang a pretty wedding song too. De food sat rite pretty on de table back at Mollie's from Sir Anderson Caterin witta big tasty cake sittin in de middle from Diane's Bakery ova in Barnesville.

De men wore sharp suits from Walter's Tuxedos in Griffin. A heep of peeple showed up, even my second grade teacher Miss Winfrey surprised me. Miss Winfrey wuz de best second grade teacher anybody could ever hav. She wore fine clothes dat I always wished I wuz ole enough to wear, all de way down to de shoes. She had long curly sandy brown hair dat looked good wit her skin complexion and she always smelled sweet like vanilla. She de only colored in town dat lived in a three story house wit a white picked fence. I's member de day she picked me to be a sunflower in de class play. Eb-body wuz happy wit dey part cept fa Tillie cause she thought she ought to been de flower. She couldn't though on de count dat she wuz taller than eb-body on de count of her bein left back in de same grade so much. Miss Winfrey made me feel pretty fa pickin me to be de flower dat day, dats why I's love sunflowers to dis day. Havin her hea to see me marry off is de best gift she could giv me. *"Sabrina, you're just as pretty as a sunflower."* She said to me as I proached de doors of de school house on my wedding day.

I wished my cousin Derrick coulda been hea but he in de Air Force, stationed in Italy; he my mama's half brotha's chile. Miss Joyce from Pretty Windas scraped up sum nice yella fabrics from her sewing sto and draped dem ova de long windas of de school house. My daddy did me good, he got one of those fancy horse carriage from Ricky's stable sittin in front of de building. My Grandmama's three beautiful sisters, Auntee Maya, Auntee Toni, and Auntee Zora cided to take a trip back down home. It wuz de biggest wedding dis town had ever seen. I didn't hav to do nuthin cause my daddy knowed folks from all ova de nawth. My flower gurls wuz angels, I wanted dem to be bare footed wit Elise leading de way. Flo babysit her sumtime when her mama hav to spend de nite at work. My two sistahs lit a candle fa de two peeple dat I grew up knowin as my mama and daddy. Furst Lady Evangelist Marilyn wuz in charge of everthang.

De winda girls stood at de winda afta my wedding party marched up de road and in de building. Ben had no idea dat I wuz gon walk up dat road to him. So when de flower gurls saw me walkin up de road, dey hollered out, *"De bride is comin, de bride is comin!"* And then dey opened de shutters so dat Ben and eb-body could see me walkin up de road. De double doors wuz closed to de building when I reached de doorway. De doors opened and there I wuz standin there, wit my daddy on my side to walk me down dat aisle. Us exchanged vows and then headed to Mollie's Juke Joint fa de reception wit me and Ben leading de way in a horse and carriage.

Johnnie Mae and Miller. I mean, mama and daddy had a bigger house build wit de money dat he sold his folks land wit, his grandma and grandpa had left de land in his name. He had to come way down from Chicago to see bout it. Ben and me spectin twins in a few months. A boy and a girl, I's already know dat he gon hav dem playin instruments.

Now, when us go to our place unda dat tree near de pond, us plannin our chilren future. He don't want me to work, so I stay home and make money keepin other folks chilren. Essie and Tim came back home finally and Po Tillie lost her mind and wuz sent away to Georgia Regional Mental Hospital. I hea talk dat she stayed long enough to meet a man. And now dey sit round de house all day makin sho dey takin dey medicine on time. I guess there's sumbody fa ebbody. Us still goes to de Juke Joint on Fridays, dey made Ray a full-time band member. Ben even hired a lady sanger by de name of Candy. All of dem is bad together, mo and mo peeple pack Mollie's eeeevery Friday. And my Ben, honey he still be all ova dat place wit dat guitar.

Eeeeeeever body loves him, but not like me. I sit there eeeevery Friday front and center starring in his eyes from my table, waitin fa de nite to end so dat when us git home I can giv him a hot oil foot and body rub, run his bath wawter. And aftawards, rest my head on his broad chest and fall to sleep to de sounds of love beatin from his heart, for me.

"The literary world must make room for Cassandra L. Thomas. This book is simply A Wonderful Read."
> **- B. Trice, Author of Echoes of My Soul**

"A beautiful way to honor our culture's history."
> **-Kitty Pope, former editor for Upscale Magazine & Author of Beside Every Man**

Cassandra L. Thomas is a former writer for Upscale Magazine residing in her native Atlanta.

Made in the USA
Charleston, SC
04 February 2013